Gloria in excelsis Deo

THE STORY OF THE FIRST CHRISTMAS

Aged 5 - 12

MIRIAM COBZA

Copyright © 2022- All rights reserved.

No part of this publication may be reproduced, distributed or transmitted in any form.

This book belongs to

_____

A long time ago, God decided to send his Son, the Saviour, to Earth to help people live happily.
He chose Mary to be the mother of his Son, a young girl from Nazareth. She was to marry Joseph who also lived in Nazareth.

When the time came, God sent the angel Gabriel to Mary in Nazareth to announce that she would be the mother of His Son, who would be called Jesus. Mary replied, "May it be according to your word". And the angel left.

The angel Gabriel also went to Joseph to tell him that Mary would become the mother of the Son of God and that he should take her as his wife. And Joseph took Mary home with him.

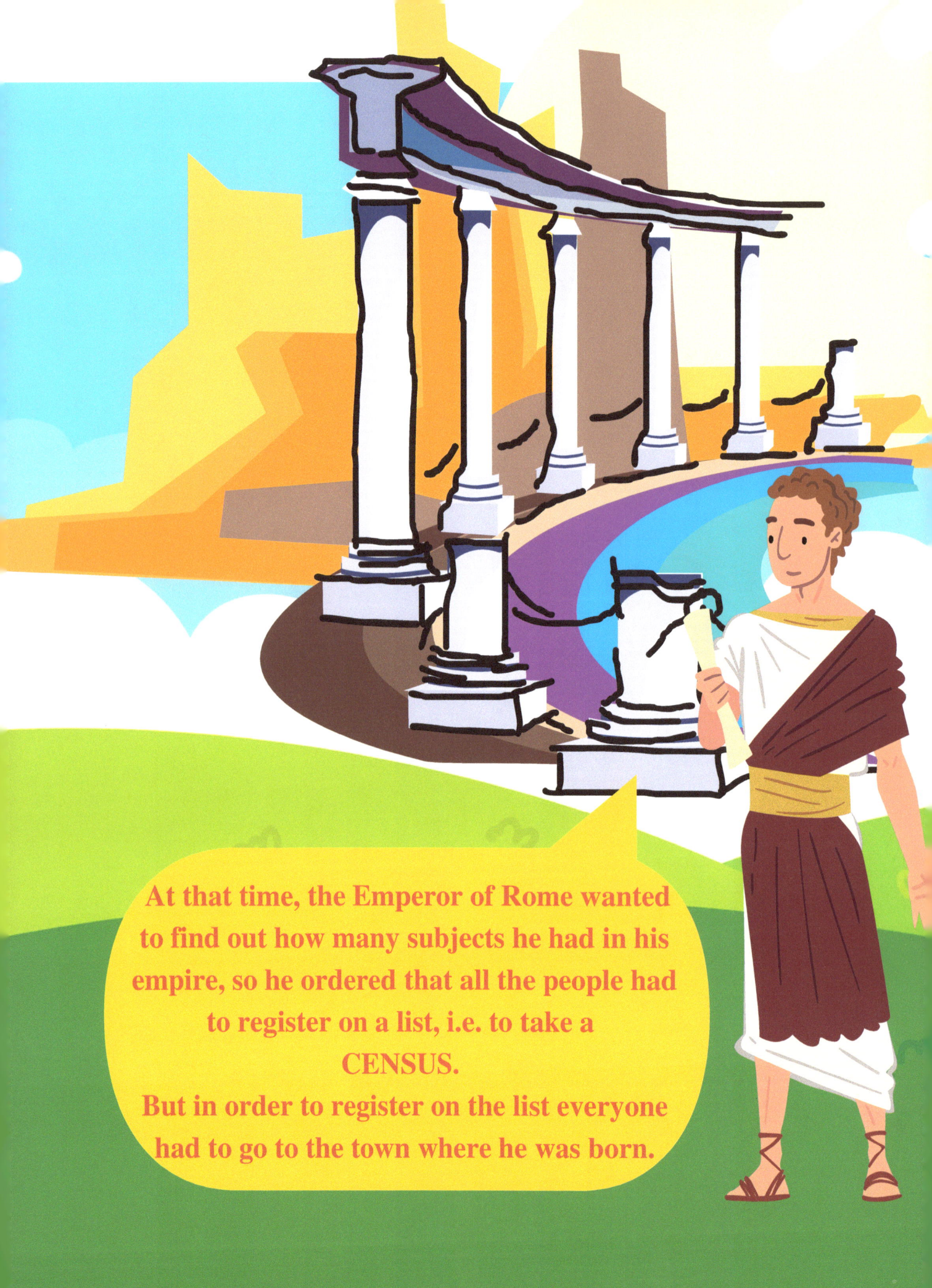

At that time, the Emperor of Rome wanted to find out how many subjects he had in his empire, so he ordered that all the people had to register on a list, i.e. to take a CENSUS.
But in order to register on the list everyone had to go to the town where he was born.

Joseph had been born in Bethlehem, so he went with Mary, who was pregnant, to register. Mary walked with difficulty, so Joseph put her on a donkey.

A few days before the birth of Jesus, the Heavenly Father chose an angel to become His messenger to go to Earth to see how His Son would be received and to write down everything that would happen on the occasion of this Event. The angel received this mission with great joy, and hurried down to Earth to do his job.

He saw Mary and Joseph on their way to Bethlehem and decided to find out what messages people had for Jesus on the occasion of His birth.

In Jesus' country it was cold, in other lands it was winter, and in other parts of the Earth it was hot. The angel saw that the people were living in their houses and that they were cold and careless. When he came to Earth, he did not find anyone to give a message to Jesus on his approaching birth day. The people of Judea were waiting for their Saviour to come down from Heaven surrounded by angels, but the Jesus who was born in Bethlehem they did not want to meet them, even though he wanted to bring them peace and love. The angel was saddened, he cried a little, his heart was heavy. Then he had an idea – to see what messages some animals had for Jesus on the eve of His coming to earth.

Leaving the jungle the angel met a group of animals and birds, who were having a meeting. He asked, "Would you like to give a message to Jesus?

The leader of the elephant family took the floor and said, "We, elephants, will make a lot of noise, we will stamp our feet and shout: <<Welcome, our Lord, to us on Earth>> so that all people may hear that today Christ is born.

The angel flew away to another part of the Earth, where it was winter. He did not meet any people, but he met other animals who were willing to send messages of welcome to the Son of God.

In an area with ice and low temperatures, he met a roe deer with her calf. The angel asked her if she had a message of greeting for the baby Jesus who would be born in Bethlehem in harsh and inhospitable conditions.

With much embarrassment and surprise at the sight of the angel, the doe replied, "With all the gentleness a baby needs, I send him a warm <<Welcome>>, and from my heart I send him much love. I greet Mary and Joseph with all my respect and congratulate them for having taken on the responsibility of being the parents of the Son of God".

The angel gladly received this generous message, thanked the doe very much and went on his way. He started heading towards Bethlehem because there was not much time left before Jesus' birth.

Flying to Bethlehem, from above, he saw a squirrel. The angel approached her and asked if she could give Jesus a birth day message. The squirrel replied:
"Yes, it is with great love and with much joy that I say to him <<Welcome to Earth, our King>>. For his parents I have a present, peanuts and walnuts".
The angel gladly received the message and the squirrel's gift and went on his way.

In his haste, the angel spotted a fox struggling to catch a fish for food. The angel asked her, "Do you have a message for Jesus?

With a melodious and meek voice, the fox answers:
"With much love I say: <<Welcome to Earth, Teacher!>> I know you will teach people to love the truth in order to be happy!"

Near Santa's house, the angel saw a reindeer ready to leave. "What message do you have for Jesus?" the angel asked him.

"Welcome, my King! for your birth on Earth has brought me the pleasure and joy of bringing gifts to children all over the Earth", the reindeer replied.

The messenger angel arrived near the town of Bethlehem and saw that Mary and Joseph had found no shelter. There were no vacancies left at the inn and no man would take them into his home. Now they were heading for the stable outside the town. Above the stable therewas a big star which would announce to all the people the birth of their Savior.

It was night. Mary and Joseph, together with their donkey, arrived at the place where they were to take shelter and where Jesus would be born. The angel was near them.

Not long after, in that place, Jesus Christ, the Son of God, was born. Mary and Joseph placed him in the manger where the animals were eating. The choirs of angels began to sing in Heavens.

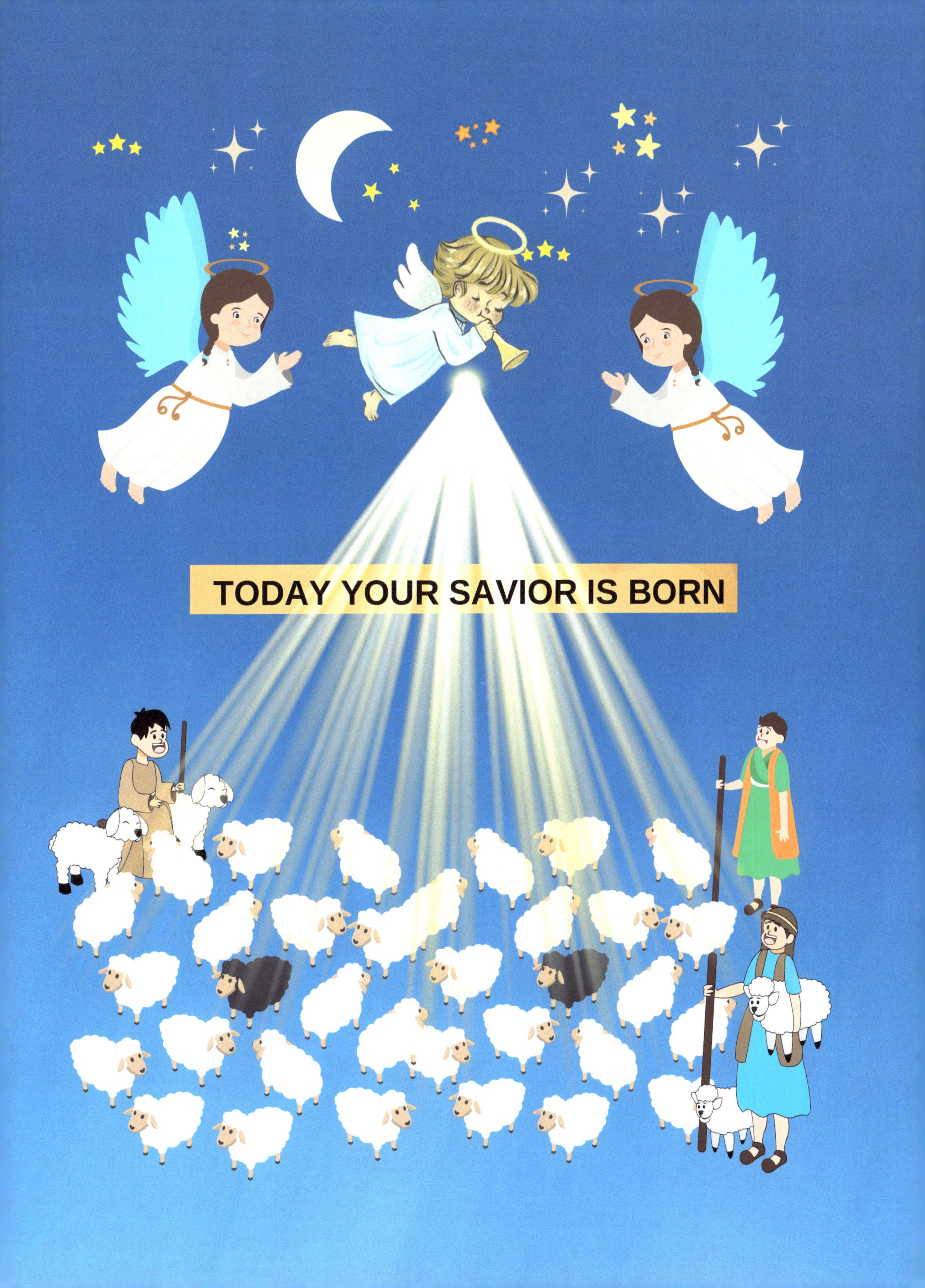
TODAY YOUR SAVIOR IS BORN

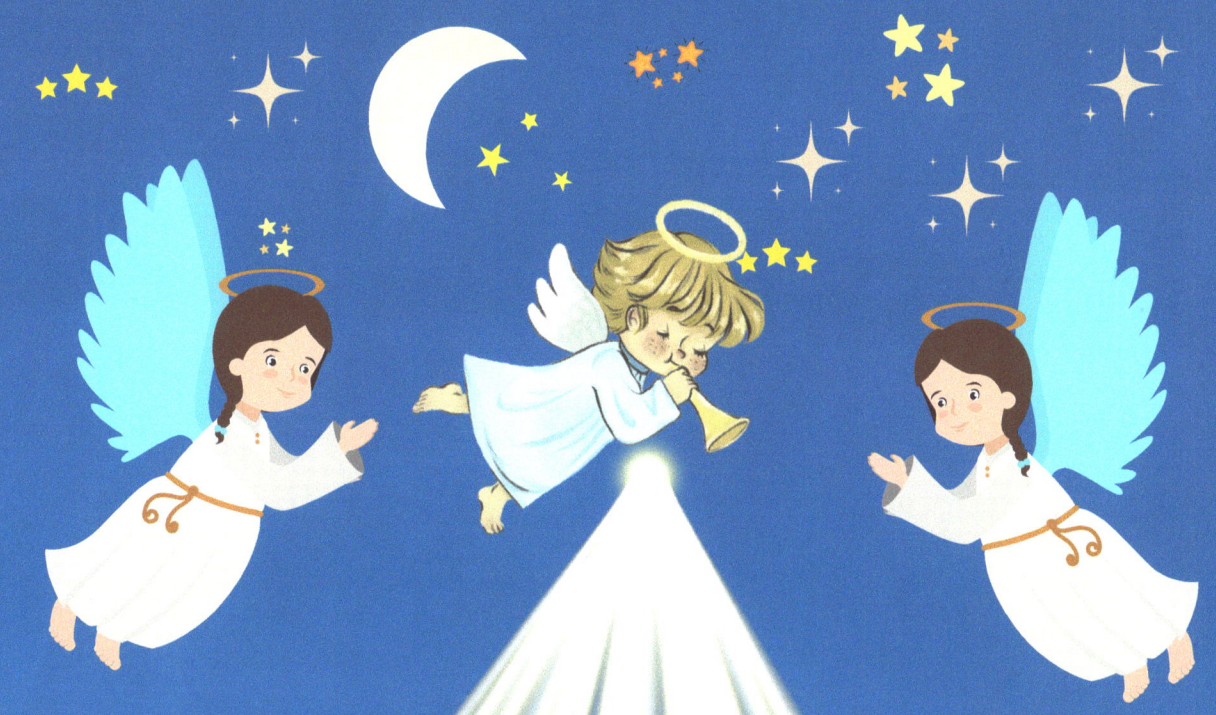

The messenger angel stayed close to Jesus, Mary and Joseph. He sensed that there would be people who would rejoice. His dream had come true. He saw how immediately after Jesus' birth, shepherds, who had been informed by other angels that their Saviour had been born, came with great joy. The shepherds believed what the angels had told them the news and went to see him. They were happy and brought Jesus a few eggs and lambs as a gift. The angel asked a shepherd:

"What message are you giving Jesus now, on the day of his birth? The shepherd answered:

"For many hundreds of years, we, people, have been waiting for You, so I thank You for coming and I am glad that I have been given the gift of seeing You. Now I will go and take the news to everyone I know".

Then the angel asked a little lamb if he had a message for Jesus. The little lamb said:

"Thank You, my Lord, for coming to Earth to be the Good Shepherd to all people.

The angel stayed close by to see what would happen in the next few days.

The angel noticed that during the day Mary and Joseph took care of Jesus with great gentleness and attention, and at night, when he was sleeping and the parents were very tired, the donkey they had come from Nazareth with and an ox were standing by the manger which served as His crib.

The angel approached them and asked them:

"Why do you stay with Jesus all night?

The ox, with his head down, said:

"We are standing here with our Lord, the King of the Universe, so that through our nostrils we may draw hot air to warm him.

The astonished angel, with great joy exclaimed:

"Yes, you have received Jesus with great kindness and generosity because you are really doing something for Him.

Would you like to give him a message for his birthday?" the angel continued.

The donkey took the floor, and with great humility said:

"With much love we say <<Welcome>> because He will help people to understand that to be happy they must help each other and have gentle and humble hearts".

The angel was impressed and very happy that Jesus, Mary and Joseph formed the Holy Family in which LOVE reigned.

Three wise men who were stargazing at night from distant lands saw the bright star that appeared in the sky and decided to follow it to reach Jesus. On the way they met each other.

But when they reached Jerusalem the star disappeared.

Then they asked Herod, king of Judea, the region where Bethlehem is located, where the newborn king was. Herod said to them, "Go and let me know when you find Him; I want to bring Him a gift!"

The Magi found Jesus and his parents. They worshipped Him and gave Him gifts of gold, myrrh and frankincense.

The messenger angel admired the selflessness and humility of the three wise men. At the same time he saw that King Herod was very angry. He believed that Jesus had come to Earth to reign as king in his place

The Magi wanted to go back to their own countries but the reporter angel told them to go another way so that they would not pass by King Herod who wanted to kill Jesus.

The angel doesn't miss the opportunity and interviews one of the Magi.

"Please tell me what is your name and what made you come from distant lands to worship the Lord Jesus?

My name is Balthasar and the other two are Gaspar and Melchior.

We, who follow the stars that the Creator has placed on the celestial vault, have seen that a star has appeared that is different from all the others and that it announces that the King of the Universe, the Son of God, has been born, the One who will bring Salvation and Change for men. He is the Light for men and those who will follow Him will know the LOVE of God".

The angel also informs Joseph that Herod wants to kill Jesus. Joseph takes Jesus and Mary and flees to another country, Egypt. The messenger angel bids farewell to Jesus, Mary and Joseph and ascends to the Heavenly Father to report all that had happened.

You, dear child, who have read this book, are one of the happy people who have the opportunity to know Jesus and to receive LOVE from Him, to give to all those around you, so that the world may become better and better!

Merry Christmas

Thank You

We hope you enjoyed our book.
As a small family company, your feedback is very important to us.
Please let us know how you like our book at
miriamcobza@gmail.com

CPSIA information can be obtained
at www.ICGtesting.com
Printed in the USA
LVHW072051051222
734228LV00034B/758